ADVANCED
PATROL
TACTICS

Skills for Today's Street Cop

Written by a Patrolman for Patrol Officers

By Michael T. Rayburn

Looseleaf
Law Publications, Inc.

43-08 162nd Street
Flushing, NY 11358
(800) 647-5547
www.LooseleafLaw.com   llawpub@erols.com

Library of Congress Cataloging-in-Publication Data

Rayburn, Michael T., 1959-
    Advanced Patrol Tactics : skills for today's street cop/ written by a patrolman for patrol officers by Michael T. Rayburn
      p. cm.
Includes index.
ISBN 1-889031-54-2
1. Police patrol. I. Title.
HV8080.P2 R39 2001
363.2'32--dc21

2001006129

Printed in U.S.A.

Cover design by: Armen Edgarian
                   armenjohn@aol.com

Dedication

This book is dedicated to my brother and sister officers who have lost their lives while in the line of duty, especially to those courageous officers who died on September 11th 2001 when the World Trade Center in New York City was attacked. This book is also dedicated to the rest of us - who are still out there making a difference. God bless America and God bless those who protect it from criminal tyranny.

The Piper

O' can you hear-
The piper as he comes nearer.
'Tis a ballad you know,
You've heard it time and again over the hedgerow.
It's the one that makes old women and young men cry,
The very same one that brings a tear to your eye.
It's an ancient song of sorrow,
One that makes us all wonder if there's hope for tomorrow.
'Tis the song they play at a funeral,
The one that's played for our fallen at burial.
The piper plays the solemn note,
The priest recites a holy quote.
The body is laid to rest,
So the piper plays his very best.
O' can you hear-
The piper as he comes nearer.
For he does not play for the dead,
But for the rest of us instead.

Michael T. Rayburn

I would like to thank Jen & Jim Cook, Tony Straus, Chris Ozolins, Patrick O' Leary and Paul Veitch for their assistance with the pictures for this book. A special thanks to EMR and BC, for without them this book would not be possible.

Another great book by *Michael T. Rayburn:*

Advanced Vehicle Stop Tactics
Skills for Today's Survival Conscious Officer

Advanced Vehicle Stop Tactics, in my opinion, is one of the most well-researched, thorough, comprehensive, easy to read and easy to understand manuals on how to conduct vehicle stops.

David M. Grossi,
Former Senior Instructor
Calibre Press, Inc.
Street Survival Seminars

Table of Contents

About the Author

Mike Rayburn started his law enforcement career on November 7th 1977 as a Military Police Officer in the United States Army. He was stationed in what was then called West Germany. Mike's assignments included working as a patrol officer, a desk sergeant, a patrol supervisor and worked undercover a number of times in the pursuit of narcotic and black market investigations.

In 1979 Mike was temporarily reassigned to S.H.A.P.E. Headquarters in Belgium. He was sent there as part of a reactionary force to secure the airfield in the wake of the terrorist bombing attack against then Supreme Allied Commander, General Alexander Haig.

After receiving an honorable discharge from the Army, Mike went to work in the private sector as a private investigator and then as a retail security manager. He was extremely proficient in the area of employee theft and was often temporarily assigned to other stores throughout the Northeast to conduct and assist other security personnel with internal investigations to resolve employee theft problems.

In 1985 Mike went to work for the U. S. Department of Justice – Federal Bureau of Prisons as a Correctional Officer. After graduating from the academy in Glynco, Georgia he was assigned to Ray Brook Correctional Facility in Ray Brook, N. Y.

In 1986 the Saratoga Springs Police Department hired Mike as a patrolman but in an undercover capacity. Saratoga Springs had an emerging crack cocaine problem and Mike was hired to try and resolve some of that problem. He worked undercover posing as a taxi cab driver and hanging out in the local bars. While undercover Mike made numerous felony arrests for narcotic sales and was responsible for the breakup and successful prosecution of a large New York City connection that was responsible for transporting large shipments of crack cocaine to Saratoga Springs.

Mike is certified by New York State as a Police Instructor, OC Instructor and Firearms Instructor. He also holds several Instructor level certificates from various companies and manufacturers in the law enforcement product field.

Mike has written a number of articles which have appeared in *Law and Order* and *Police Magazine*. He is a recognized expert in the areas of officer safety, vehicle stops, and firearms tactics and training. This is Mike's second book. His first book titled, "Advanced Vehicle Stop Tactics: Skills for Today's Survival Conscious Officer" was released in the spring of 2001. Numerous police academies have adopted "Advanced Vehicle Stop Tactics" as a "must read" training manual for their recruits.

Mike has recently released his first training video titled, "Instinctive Point Shooting with Mike Rayburn." This is a "must have" video for any officer who is serious about their safety and is interested in realistic firearms tactics.

Mike is also the owner and lead instructor of Rayburn Law Enforcement Training (R. L. E. T.). Rayburn Law Enforcement Training is a professional organization that provides comprehensive training programs to local, state, military and federal law enforcement officers. His courses include Advanced Vehicle Stops, Instinctive Point Shooting and Instinctive Point Shooting Instructor. To obtain information about Mike's training video or any of his classes contact him by E-mail at: RLET1@AOL.com.